# TREVOR LAWRENCE

L STAR

By Douglas Lynne

Book design by Jake Nordby
Cover design by Jake Nordby

Photographs ©: Matt Patterson/AP Images, cover, 1; Tom DiPace/AP Images, 4, 16, 23; David Rosenblum/Icon Sportswire, 6–7; Phelan M. Ebenhack/AP Images, 9; Hyosub Shin/Atlanta Journal-Constitution/AP Images, 10; John Byrum/Icon Sportswire, 12; Scott Strazzante/San Francisco Chronicle/AP Images, 15; Michael Owens/AP Images, 18; Kevin Sabitus/AP Images, 21; Red Line Editorial, 22

Press Box Books, an imprint of Press Room Editions.

**Library of Congress Control Number: 2023909336**

**ISBN**
978-1-63494-759-6 (library bound)
978-1-63494-766-4 (paperback)
978-1-63494-779-4 (epub)
978-1-63494-773-2 (hosted ebook)

Distributed by North Star Editions, Inc.
2297 Waters Drive
Mendota Heights, MN 55120
www.northstareditions.com

Printed in the United States of America
102023

# ABOUT THE AUTHOR

Douglas Lynne is a freelance writer. He spent many years working in the media, first in newspapers and later for online organizations, covering everything from breaking news to politics to entertainment to sports. He lives in Minneapolis, Minnesota.

# TABLE OF CONTENTS

# 1

# TIME TO SHINE

Trevor Lawrence took the snap, dropped back, and was sacked. Things kept getting worse for the Jacksonville Jaguars. The team had picked Lawrence first in the 2021 National Football League (NFL) Draft. Most experts viewed the quarterback as a sure-thing star. But midway through his second year, he had yet to show it.

**Trevor Lawrence prepares to throw a pass in a 2022 game against the Baltimore Ravens.**

Lawrence scans the field for an open receiver.

The Jaguars started the 2022 season 3-7. Now they trailed the Baltimore Ravens 27-20. After the sack, only 1:51 remained in the

game. The Jags needed to go 86 yards for a touchdown. Jacksonville faced third and 21.

Nothing was going to rattle Lawrence on this sunny Florida afternoon. The 6-foot-6 quarterback completed a 16-yard pass. Then, on fourth down, he threw for 10 more yards. The Jaguars were on their way.

Soon they moved to the 10-yard line. Only 20 seconds remained. Lawrence fired the ball into the corner. Receiver Marvin Jones snagged it for a touchdown.

An extra point would have tied the game. Instead, the Jags put the ball back in Lawrence's hands. He delivered with another perfect throw for two points.

Lawrence's clutch fourth-quarter performance secured a 28–27 win. Finally, he was playing like a franchise quarterback. He was only getting started.

### BIG THROWS

Trevor Lawrence completed 15 of 19 passes for 173 yards and 2 touchdowns in the fourth quarter. Two of those completions came on fourth down. He helped his team score 18 points in the final quarter and sparked a come-from-behind win.

Lawrence celebrates with wide receiver Marvin Jones after throwing a touchdown pass to him.

CANES

# 2

# CLEMSON KING

Trevor Lawrence was born on October 6, 1999, in Knoxville, Tennessee. However, he grew up in Cartersville, Georgia, a small city near Atlanta. By middle school, Trevor was turning heads as a quarterback. His football instincts were spectacular. Plus, he was already 6-foot-2.

Trevor became a superstar at Cartersville High School. He set

**Trevor Lawrence led his high school football team to two Georgia state championships.**

Lawrence posted a 38-2 record as a quarterback at Clemson University.

Georgia state records for passing yards and touchdowns. In 54 starts, he won 52 games. Strangers lined up for autographs. More than 100 college coaches came to watch him play. Experts considered Trevor the country's top high school player. Many expected him to choose the University of Georgia. It was just 100 miles from where he lived. Instead, Trevor decided to play for Clemson University in South Carolina.

Clemson was a big-time program when Lawrence arrived in 2018. The Tigers had been national champions two years earlier. And they had a good starting quarterback in Kelly Bryant. At first, Bryant and Lawrence shared time at quarterback. But after four games, Lawrence took over as the starter. Clemson was already 4–0. Under Lawrence, the team only got better. He could beat defenses by passing or running. Clemson kept on winning.

## PB&J TIME

Trevor Lawrence had been skinny all his life. He wanted to gain weight to get stronger, but nothing seemed to work. After his freshman season, he figured it out. Eating lots of peanut butter and jelly sandwiches did the trick.

The Tigers met Alabama for the national title. Both teams were undefeated. Some experts called Alabama's team the best in college football history. But after the game, everyone was talking about Lawrence. He threw for 347 yards and three touchdowns as Clemson dominated, 44–16. That performance capped one of the best freshman seasons in college football history.

Lawrence was even better as a sophomore. Once again, he led Clemson to an undefeated regular season. However, his team fell to Louisiana State University in the national title game.

Clemson was back in the playoff the next year too. This time they fell short of the title game. But Lawrence was runner-up for the Heisman Trophy, an award given to the best player in college football. Now he was ready for the NFL.

Lawrence passed for 10,098 yards in three years of college football.

JAX
16
C
NFL
16
16

3

# FRANCHISE QB

NFL fans had been eyeing Trevor Lawrence since his freshman year at Clemson. Many believed he had the tools to be an all-time great pro quarterback. In 2021, he finally got a chance to prove it. The Jacksonville Jaguars selected him with the first pick in the NFL Draft.

The Jaguars were coming off a miserable 1–15 season in 2020. Their fortunes didn't improve much in 2021.

**Lawrence can beat defenses by passing and by running with the football for big gains.**

Lawrence dives over defenders and reaches out to score a touchdown against the New York Jets.

Under first-year coach Urban Meyer, the Jaguars were a mess. Lawrence threw a league-high 17 interceptions compared to just 12 touchdowns. The team finished 3–14.

A new coach, Doug Pederson, took over in 2022. But the Jaguars continued to struggle, starting 3–7. However, fans began to notice changes in Lawrence. Pressure from defenses didn't seem to bother him as much. He was completing more of his passes and throwing fewer interceptions. Then he led the comeback win against the Baltimore Ravens. Suddenly the

### THANK YOU, JACKSONVILLE

Trevor Lawrence and Marissa Mowry married in April 2021. The NFL Draft took place soon after. Jaguars fans expected their team to select Lawrence. So they purchased the couple a toaster as a wedding gift. Then they raised $11,000 for charities of the couple's choice. As a thank-you, the newlyweds donated $20,000 to local charities.

Jaguars were red hot. A 6–1 finish to the season put them in the playoffs.

The playoffs began terribly. Lawrence threw four first-half interceptions. Jacksonville trailed the Los Angeles Chargers 27–0. Lawrence said it was the worst half he'd ever played. Then he played what might have been his best half.

Lawrence began zipping passes all over the field. Instead of throwing interceptions, he threw touchdowns. Beginning late in the second quarter, he led four straight touchdown drives. A field goal on the last play of the game secured an amazing 31–30 comeback win. Lawrence had arrived. The future in Jacksonville had never looked brighter.

## TREVOR LAWRENCE
### CAREER PASSING STATISTICS

- **2021** – 3,641 yards, 12 TDs, 17 interceptions
- **2022** – 4,113 yards, 25 TDs, 8 interceptions

Lawrence celebrates after leading his team to victory in the playoffs.

# TIMELINE MAP

1. **Knoxville, Tennessee: 1999**
   Trevor Lawrence is born on October 6.
2. **Cartersville, Georgia: 2017**
   Lawrence wraps up his prep career at Cartersville High School, where he set multiple state records.
3. **Clemson, South Carolina: 2018**
   Lawrence takes over as Clemson's starter in the fifth game of his freshman season. The Tigers defeat Syracuse 27–23 on September 29.
4. **Santa Clara, California: 2019**
   Lawrence leads Clemson to a 44–16 win over Alabama on January 7 to claim the national title.
5. **New Orleans, Louisiana: 2020**
   Lawrence and Clemson fall to Louisiana State in the national title game on January 13.
6. **Cleveland, Ohio: 2021**
   On April 29, the Jacksonville Jaguars select Lawrence with the first overall pick in the NFL Draft.
7. **Jacksonville, Florida: 2021**
   After losing his first five starts, Lawrence wins his first NFL game when the Jaguars beat the Miami Dolphins 23–20.
8. **Jacksonville, Florida: 2023**
   Lawrence leads the Jaguars to a 31–30 playoff victory over the Los Angeles Chargers after trailing 27–0 in the first half.

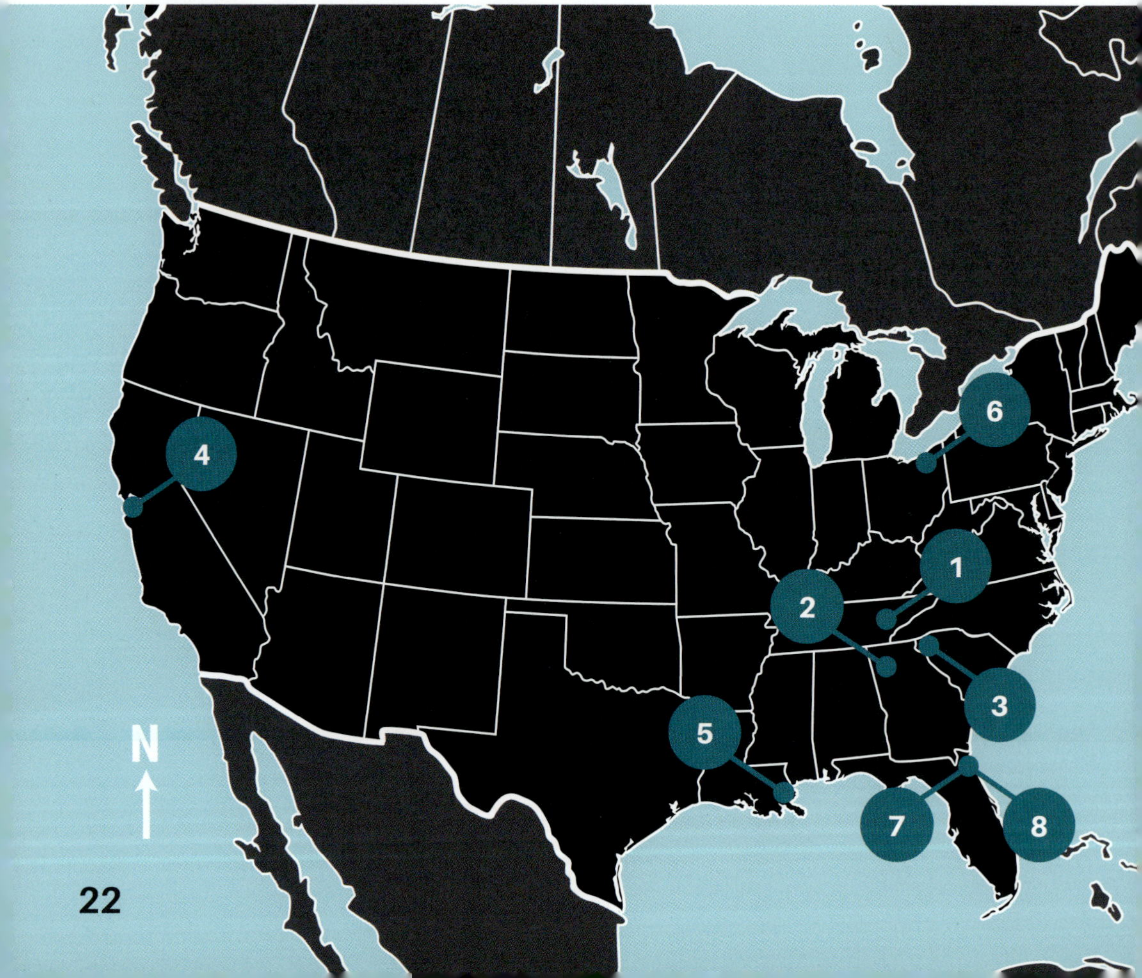

# AT-A-GLANCE

## TREVOR LAWRENCE

**Birth date:** October 6, 1999

**Birthplace:** Knoxville, Tennessee

**Position:** Quarterback

**Height:** 6 feet 6 inches

**Weight:** 213 pounds

**Current team:** Jacksonville Jaguars (2021-)

**Past team:** Clemson Tigers (2018-20)

**Major awards:** ACC Offensive Player of the Year (2020), ACC Player of the Year (2020), Pro Bowl (2022)

*Accurate through the 2022 season.*

# MORE INFORMATION

To learn more about Trevor Lawrence, go to **pressboxbooks.com/AllAccess**.

These links are routinely monitored and updated to provide the most current information available.

# GLOSSARY

### charities
Organizations that help people in need.

### clutch
Having to do with a difficult situation when the outcome of the game is in question.

### draft
An event that allows teams to choose new players coming into the league.

### franchise quarterback
A star quarterback expected to lead a team for several years.

### instincts
Natural ways of thinking.

### sack
A tackle of the quarterback behind the line of scrimmage.

# INDEX